Emotions, Images, and Spirit

Early Collected Poems 1963-1971

by David A. Folds

Copyright © 2018 by David A. Folds

All rights reserved.

No part of this book may be reproduced or transmitted in any form or by any means, electronic or mechanical, including photocopying, recording or by any information storage and retrieval system, without written permission from the author, except for the inclusion of brief quotations in review.

Published in the United States and the United Kingdom

by WingSpan Press, Livermore, CA

The WingSpan name, logo and colophon are the trademarks of WingSpan Publishing.

ISBN 978-1-59594-618-8

First edition 2018

Printed in the United States of America

www.wingspanpress.com

Library of Congress Control Number 2018934329

1 2 3 4 5 6 7 8 9 10

Emotions, Images, and Spirit

THIS IS DEDICATED

TO MY FATHER, THOMAS (TOM)

AND

MY MOTHER, KATHERINE (KITTY)

WHO GAVE MORE TO ME

DURING THIS TIME

THAN I COULD GIVE BACK TO THEM

(HOPEFULLY I GAVE MORE LATER)

Clarity

a never painted

you   a dry

warm mist

my eyes seem

to penetrate but

never catch

you standing there

a still-shot in

my memory

1963 - NYC

Cloud Eclipse

a cloud-filled gray

overhead   expanding its beams

covering me and around I miss

the gradual loss of grey

an irregular line of light gliding

to me along green turned brownish

ground stirring the air to new

life   somehow I miss

the approach   I feel the touch

of the grey I feel

a transformation I too

am stirred by the light

caught unaware   I look

not to the sun a cloud still covers it

but I feel you close to me

1963 - NYC

Eyes That Smile

    I knew in a day

of roses not so red not

the sun in an hour

    of questions all unheard and said

the answer with deaf-ears

1963 - NYC

Cinemation

looking out on a wide

expanded screen   I saw

a technicolored black pitch

in a three-dimensional theater

of life with an eye's mind   and thought

the stars below far brighter

1963 - NYC

Deep Steps Retraced

I put the tips of my fingers

on my forehead the slight tingling touch

of the trail they follow somehow

forces my eyes to close my eyelids

seeing the bright darkness within my memory

searching this darkness for your image

my fingers retrace the path

yours once engraved on my senses

1963 - NYC

Inhalation of Yesterday

there was a song sung

    once ago I heard it

  murmured by a soft wind

  gone in a half shadowed half

dying yard swarmed by walls too high

 too far about   my chest

    held much familiar air imprisoned

for this so silent song my muscles taut

not one move or quiver awaiting once

  again that never more heard echo

1963 - NYC

Fonts Baptismaux

In days when rainbows scoured

the skies of rains that greyed

and wet   the multiglowing

thoughtful tints took one long stride

sweeping so immense and cleansed me

of all once-tenacious memories

1963 - NYC

Scattered Thoughts

inhaling atmospheres of sweat

the coolness of the evening frustrates now

a warmth that vibrates faintly soft

heavy sounds half of sighs, half-breaths

disrupt a clearer stillness and some thoughts

of am I somehow not the same

is it possible I've changed

and yet two legs remain uncovered

1963 - NYC

Photo Fragments

each slight turn of the wind

    each weak current lifts them up

moves them   rearranges   some turn over

few touch waiting a next wind to separate

    but the image stays   a smile

almost laughing   at me?   at her?

it mesmerizes my fingers it contracts them

    nails eating into soft skin

    scattered by another wind

   new shape   new places   but the image

    laughs and my arms shake

and I feel a slight wind move me

1963 - NYC

The Golden Fleece

I looked past the sun

further   beyond a dazzling

burning sigh   revolving

spinning, dancing lights—a multitude

merging into one   breathing a radiance

that warmed my face

that laughed with my skin

to a tingling touch   a laughter

heard by inner ears   a playful hand

that beckoned me   far past

a smiling face

1963 - NYC

In Memory

it never quite seems real

as I think about it

later each detail moves about each

a gaseous substance freely expanding

contracting in a whirl in a twisting wind

able to intertwine with

another   each forming a mist

about the other my thoughts can

only sense that you had once

been there but still

I'm never really sure

1963 - NYC

The Uncontemplative

a wave rising on its haunches

smashed against concrete still unconquered

exploding   destroyed in drenches of spray

needles of wetness darting everywhere

another charge   gliding towards destruction

familiar and yet not knowing

the collision with my senses

the reverberating cry

1963 - NYC

Nocturnal

over streaming velvet green

undulating   gradually sloping lower

lower far below a level gaze

a hypnotic   demanding sight

over green rolling velvet

past breakers failing to climb

to rise to an always dry summit

to escape the sight of two distant sails

white on deep gleaming blue   they claim

the caress of my sight the laugh

the gleam in my slave-held eyes

over green velvet sleeping still

1963 - NYC

Amortized

seen there

the turning

spinning extent which

my senses had swayed

    her   how she stood

but supported by motion

the motion of my influence

cried her moving form

must topple yet or

I must be denied then

sent away

1964 - NYC

Past

the last one time

I saw her the last unless

as I saw her   smiling silently

in memory she could see

my smile   vaguer perhaps

but existing   more than she

than ever she saw my inward

laughter

expanding gradually

1964 - NYC

Evolution

in the last days of a world

turned sideways

figures passed gliding

with flowing flesh lines

one slight move

to set in motion a breast

a buttocks and all mine to see

and think of all mine before

the past of my world

turned sideways

1964 - NYC

Myopic

in the quiet of shadows

a passing car

on another street   the movement

of the taut seat-springs

fierce breaths

as she waited

the short pause

I sensed was necessary

1964 - NYC

False Hopes

the life in turn will

    laugh

        as I once

    in finding

        my pain a comic

not to be serious not one

        among a layer

            of frustrations

1964 - NYC

Journey

   if

       a wind flows a breeze

     lifts me   transports

   me   away

     it's as if I

       had never

stirred your hand

        near mine

   still that way

1964 - NYC

Spoken

somewhere a soft sound

a whisper

    far from me I knew it

clearly still a verbal moon-

light waning

    slightly my thoughts could strain

        to wonder what,

but   no

only hear —

    the beauty in   the thought

    that yet remembers that

    yet can taste

        to savor it

listening

    still in stillness

the words have left behind

1964 - NYC

Hidden

    that was not me

           my arm

  you grasped

                protecting

    your sweet life the Eden

      naïve as my love as

               you saying

  you didn't know

      knowing   I'm sure but

               never forming

  the words to tell

        your lips and me

the last days

        betrayed both

and told

1964 - NYC

Thorns

mending yesterday

    was not so fine

Greg-Gory had (as yet)

  and still not returned

Martha may I then?------

      and the twice

  and then the third

      (my head still throbs)

can yesterdays still return?

        between your sobs

  whispers never

see themselves never

      swim within

and you

      speak so softly

and would think

must this one whisper too?

sometimes I kick

           things---

  bellow, belch

coarseness sometimes runs

      through me (don't you know

I've got to build things) and

      mending yesterday was

hard (I know) running against the

           grain

1964 - NYC

Apparitions

    the day is not

  yet

     I knew it in

her eyes   thoughts pass

           like

    pastoral scenes viewed

   from a pullman

car whole choruses

      for her have

not yet been

         sung

    thoughts float

 like   many

  -colored mists (you laugh

at me)

     ideas are

 still unknown as

    once undeveloped

  breasts

   behind me now

 night now   still unseen

   (I can't look

back)

   huge hands hover

threatening

        and are gone

    leaving

           only an unsure

       promise that they

             might (perhaps)

return

      one slight shadow

    moved

           thoughts sparked

      to kindling

      brought forth

          a combustion

and

        my mind Explodes!

but after

the mushroomed destroyer

softer ideas

of dust

hung

in an

atmosphere

of memories

poignant melancholia

my own

flower its fertile petals

stroke

my forehead filling

my eyes with

sterile seed

and lasting

impressions past

a flickering

David A. Folds

    silent film seen

        through a torrent of

            downward

    slanting rain

        incomplete scenes

    jagged

        halting movement not quite

            real anymore

    and hands feel

        smooth

    the surface celluloid cleansed

        rain washed filmed

            plasma

    a dimension short

        of touch and

            me

1965 - NYC

The Shifting-Time of My Own Psyche

the different dances

the lyrics

sung sometimes shouted

some a

whisper are far

more surprising than the

red-greens

of irregular

traffic lights of

Generalizations   what next?

who's to tell –

the shift that sets

tomorrow's stage

1965 - NYC

Reverie

                                                  lending shadows

               we two

                        walked

     darkening pavement   sidewalk

                              curb

                        street

                       shadows meet

            briefly kiss

                     hold   hug

             grasp a

                     bliss without a

      touch   passed by cars

                 alive

                     passing people past

        away from you

            my thoughts all

                ask

              we knew

we two   but

                where was

        flesh

1965 - NYC

Devils Dance

my mind

retarded   not by

the difficulty of the

ellipses of reason the arc

of tolerance sweeping

viciously

in the motion of

a still-shot

not

by the proud

dwarf of civilization

proud parody of

progress   yours perhaps

not mine

not by our

    bleeding buildings that

          pierce past clouds

they too   a mist

      easily dispersed but

  this last morning

  my eyes laughed

        and

      did a dance

     with bright

    phosphorous

  clowns

of light singing:

"...and is this all there is?"

1965 - NYC

Village Vagrant

      in spite

     of laughter

    around his void

of humor his vacuum

         of self-scorn

the rigidity of his pathos

          remains

a face powerless

     to now throw forth

an expression

       hinting at a world

        of comedy

1966 - NYC

Song to Her Dusk

the sun

        spoken in soft

hair caresses the bleached white

        of a pillow

        of a smoothed shoulder

    drops from a height

    descending

        curves downward

   chased by my concave hand

stroking as if to capture

        brightness

searching her---the sun

      to find the path

      of redescent

1966 - NYC

Triad From Past Prose

love

is smut cleansed

on sundays by

the maid

so She said

Love is before

we dirty the sheets

–her

Love is

a cleansed soul

irrespective of

seed and sweat

and sheets   but

without them the

teeth of my soul

would not chew

well   –me

1966 - NYC

A New Tune Introduced

        my mind again

    responds

      to the hope in loving

           laughter

heard distant to my fears

   my inward

         reaching spheres

    sovereign but curious

  of an act

that seems to jump

     all confines

  rudely jolting

    inhibitions

1966 - NYC

First Snow

as

the door opened

withdraws

the curtain revealing

I too

stop

bewildered by the

immensity of invading

white by

the occasional bit

of snow

that has caught

some of the sun's

joy dancing with it

but

    unlike me   Sukero with

  uncollared excitement leaps

    forward burying

                  self in snow

                        first

    captured then leaps

among drifts licking new friends

      laughing her own

 way and then

             to leave her

             calling-card

1966 - NYC

The Mind at Night Moments

1. Awaiting

    the naked sing

    twice the song

  I sing

my half closed

    mouth trembles no shout

no silence no

      one withheld thought

a companion to quiet

        days dawn each

  rising sun   –then let night

        squeeze out each

small light

      dripping

      from each finger

        until

                  at mid-noon of

           night   thought now

         fully partitioned

            by surged

                  dark clouds

      pauses

    yawns   –loosens jowls

            negligent

      to a cursed apathy

                sleeping in a void

                 of sleeplessness

         the silence

   of shadowed

              midnight trees

       repeats

     itself   –darkened forms

          in diversion hush

quiet dialogue

awaiting

new aspects

of a menacing

calm

of specters

—a calm

whose phantoms

strike through silence

changing nothing but

the threat

of chaos

passing without a flick

of a numbed

wind of a

dried breeze

2. Sleep

a cool tide

        rewashes

    fading pains

its ocean's stroke

        returns

soothing

   half-hidden fears shadowed

          blue liquid

   envelops

   thought eclipsed

      by a deep sleep

      bright points

        of light

    blink on tips

of a quiet sea

      caught in one

moment of a slight

      ripple to an

           easy summit

      each movement

      an instant's dance over

every

        grave-like darkening

hush

       but

         between the tips

a cooled moon-light

     skims the glazed

       sea surface

tells a whispered

       bedtime story

sings a ruffled lullaby

    leaving

       a residue

   of unfiltered innuendoes

        and down

   down below

           the gleaming surface

        each lower step

    one more gradation

       of greying

           –quiet things

glide among silent

  mildewed slime

in a re-echo

     of a past

   forgotten

echo's frown

3. 42nd and 5th

in a forestry

of books in a central

        library

of collected hieroglyphics

        once beaten

rhythmically

sheeted wood strips

        I sit waiting

in turn   my chance

        for communion with

but a few

        chosen

        declamatory anthems

                    the silence

        of dulled thought   circulates

            through dust-filled

    atmosphere

                    unaware of the waste

        of unused volumes   –not

                        intimidated by the

                    immensity

            of a room that even

                        whispers

                    with a loud voice

            that cries with

                a barking

                        cough

    as

        in a two-dimensional

            cathedral

            an austere

                    composition

halts quivering

        air currents

–aftermath

        of a pipe organ's last

shrill blast and

non-essential man sits

    within

    seated there

        within man's mind

sharp ripples stroke

the conscious surface

of a flooded

        chamber a rising

bubble an alive sign

of a submerged

    already breathless

thought enclosed in a watery

inner chilled tomb

4. Exit

–later

I return

to the wind

the outside static form

unprotected

holding itself taut

tantalized

by each fierce gust

with a whistled laugh

passed

1966 - NYC

The Next Corner Turned

that hand –mine

moves as if

to ask the arm

it slides along

is that flesh hers

now mine that soft

forearm caressed

so close to a turning elbow

feels of heat but

does not throb the coldness of

an elbow's bone jolts

my thoughts sharp piercing

soft sentiment

turned the corner

fears that upper arm

1966 - NYC

Lament

   Jenny is

       dead the overturned once

          half-buried stone uncovers

             disturbed life

     moist

   earth clung to a rock

       like the sea slime

    on a ship's bottom   –two

         grass blades

     peek out

watch a dazed worm search

a new home around a new

underside of a rock that looks

    strangely cold

   wet in a drying

         sun

    jenny is dead

1966 - NYC

A New Playing

    winds shift in

             slow sequence

  each approaching

       follows another arriving quietly

    as though embarrassed

of some slight unmentionable thought

            moving into place

  on a stage   set to

          dance from a script

  that has never been

        written

   but given

        down to

            memory for each

  waiting generation

1967 - NYC

Myself

    a light tower's dim

                bell toll

    past the searching beam

       slips through

    fog-moist air

      pummeled by fierce

sea squalls   it

       hoists its own

            bright sail

  and dances in the wind

1967 - NYC

Quick Winter Visit

Nostalgia

    still a fast passing

        face an old cord

pulled

      brought down the flush

of a mental wash

    halts all

  reason   other thoughts

leaving only--------my god

          was that----

      it can't

    be what's-her-name

1967 - NYC

Songs of Soft Map Readings

        hands

    across soft

           flesh lands

trace a course for tomorrow's

   lines and find the source

 melodic life   to hear

          the songs

   of long-held notes

 that slide about

            beneath

my touch   determined by

 a sense's tune that claims

   its vital copyright

1968 - NYC

David A. Folds

Foundations of Silence

1. Recognition

I watch the pulp

of my blood

drip

rich pools

turquoise and vermilion

which hands cannot

divide or wash or smear

engulf like quicksand

all forms

that come to call –

wing of a moth

grass blade

hair

cautious

on soft toes

    I would step

        around it to avoid

            sure capture and death

–or life

        but expanding

            in quiet certainty

        it begins to follow me

2. Microscopic

              once more

            the weaving begins

        to form a fabric out of days

           hours

              part of the tint

                  of a strand

            minutes-----only fragments

but when interwoven threads

            should combine

                for rich mixed

    colors and tight drawn textures

    my eyes still linger

    over a single

        dropped stitch

3. Again

    now the fine grained

    bits of coffee

    drop

    in a hot spring

cup   dispersing bubbles

        quietly

they form

    a new substance

which will force me to

    awaken and perhaps

    this day won't

    be quite so bad

4. Final

        and with dark times

        night also

        intrudes------------the wide span

        of its menacing right hand

        lowers itself tent-like

        as day's last lights

            try to hide

only to be forced out

        into distant exile

        while each crimson shadowed

            finger of night

        closes the fast dimmed

                gap

1968 - NYC

Mesmerism

      and in spite of all

    Spring explodes

    in a renaissance of greeting

      yes--------Nature turning

        its annual trick captures

us   in an all

            too seductive web

    –a web in which

        I must perform

    sundry

        long lost action

            –a deep

breath of air   ballad

    of the panorama of

        sun-lit green

smell of the housecleaning

of all outdoors

–and knowledge

that like nature I too

might be

rediscovered   led

into another

chance blossoming

1968 - NYC

Vertigo in June

      in full view

of the multiple

          miniature scenes

the shiny works of

    other men   I sit

high on top of a personal

    observation post---watching

    in silence waiting

for the end

    of one more bout of

        elevation sickness

tightening my grip

on a meandering

        unreliable support

1968 - NYC

Recluse

in the park of grassed

seas of green

formations of leaves flirt

with all the heated

groping air

while each move

opens a new

fact of light

a new lane cleared

through the leaves of trees

to bounce brightness

off a few

crushed blades

1968 - NYC

I Starve

the long wounds

of soft thoughts

are here again   silent

problems return

to me familiar and yet

different

like a new day

hungry but bleak

overhead

a dull-blade fan

plays with air

fiercely but nothing changes

and warm sticky drops

of sweat

slowly lower themselves

          for one moment

    seemingly the ethereal finger-tips

      of a past nemesis   now

          a still-born thought

and light has entered

    also without a sign of motion

        a lucid structured

  architecture   painted

with the dots of aroused dust particles

    a changing pattern

dropping

        to an anchored base of

    settled dust

  –measure of when

    last cleansed happiness

      overwhelmed me

1968 - NYC

Some Blues

all

the blues of the morning

taken

    aside   washed

of its bitter tints

is still

low-down

a dirty shame

and

a joy

to make a song about

afterwards

1968 - NYC

Drafted Sorrow

fright in the eyes of them

    and some are husbands

        of ballads

of billow smooth clouds

horizons

   lost in intermission   but

    in the sky flies the hawk

sharp talons…….beak –

  –swoops

   sudden attack below

       pre-storm clouds

    that roll in a darkened

 vaulted sky

     enclosing the slaughter

of men's last loved

        illusions

1968 - NYC

David A. Folds

On Nil's Beach

asking me a lifeless view

(my wide

swept

stilled panorama,

breathing still)

of heated sand

and gravel skies dead

microgametes

floating in the tide

silence laughs alone

pulse of the sea

                  now

      nothing swims

                      or drowns or cares

            or cares   **pulse gone**

                from our sea

              cadavers

                      on the beach

1968 - NYC

Returning

dawn is the soft candle stretching out

to inbetweens

light air brings to me early howls

fierce moves of metro town

tight head pulls

a loose body

til all is stretched   pulled further

and everybody sinks low to quiet

but

the rush moves through fast

skull crushing

dull force

and everybody's

spaced out

shrinking melting low

1968 - NYC

Escalators

    time

        is loosening its

        death-hold on me

days drown the night

                in life

and the walls sigh open their gills

      to exhale

                stale used-up breath

and draw in painted visions

            of nows and maybes of

        ----yes, everything

1969 - NYC

Electric Song

    I've taken off goodbyes since yesterday

and now with greetings fallen lower

    blue-tipped love slowly slides away and

        I wonder if I'm lost again

    am I going someplace fast or slow?

   well   others speed

        but I just can't slow down

with distant sounds –

        a whistle and a train

but they don't catch up

    and I just won't jump either

floating sad-eyed   empty

I think about marie and diamond skies

some truth is in the alley but

each has its own sad way of strangling

and breathing is a thing we scarcely know

and dying is a place we always go

1968 - NYC

Chemical Memory

among soft human waves

flesh thoughts   roll

drawing me under, again

but within each ebb and flow

small reminders

awaken bits of warm love

once believed gone –

banished by fierce will

      no

    not chance

        not the grit

        within a mind that

        can structure battles

(with only doubt present as witness)

      would stop

          my matador thrust touch

        its chance for truth again

1968 - NYC

Rigor Mortis

images of death flushed with

pass in quick softness

–intruders to the senses

thought uneasy before them

a choking moment

the spirit with a surface fragility

is halted

breath grows rare in a morgue

eyes remain fixed before them

morbidity overwhelms disgust

a dying stare

limp   without a pulse

remains

see the sadness with man

incapable of his capacities

unaware of his fire

        thought in monotone

        love in four letters

    realize the harsh

        curious fact of life

          (of most lives)

that it takes a lifetime

        of dying

to reach a quiet death

1969 - NYC

Maelstrom

now the doorway

is open

we walk on through

and

scatter each dusty roach

with a stride

towards our own outside

downstairs from our times

all the stories drop

off the railing and

search out the older

quiet places

–it's the anarchy of the poor

      ...said Williams

but we know

it's not, it's not that at all

    their empty prisms are

    the only could-be gods

while our shadows

    record the mass

and finger

the stain-glass   female walls

    all about tomorrow

the poems you love to touch

    and sleep

1969 - NYC

1971 New Jersey Meditation

Old half-moons revolve in time

    instead of laughter after whines.

Along the water on the trail

    the peace is flowing, floating frail.

As on the Ganges in the dusk

    we walk alone together free

        towards our master's purest peace.

Pilgrims of the world, but not complete,

    one foot planted one foot free.

Every song must have an end

    except the soul's eternal Aum.

All of life is passing by,

    hardly a breath, a second's sigh.

The mind is dead, the body, too

All that's carnal, all that grew

    is past decay, will waste away,

Except in life where we don't know

    what is balanced, what will flow.

Oldest song revolve along,

    return our peace, our oldest grace

        or teach our lives to find the place,

to be the ladders for our souls

        to climb to heights beyond our minds,

        to be the masters of our goals

For if the soul can show the way

        the path must reach eternity.

God is with us, now we with him,

        complete the circle, repeat the Aum.

1971 - NYC

Index of Poems by Titles

1971 New Jersey Meditation	80
A New Playing	52
A New Tune Introduced	37
Amortized	14
Apparitions	24
Chemical Memory	74
Cinemation	4
Clarity	1
Cloud Eclipse	2
Deep Steps Retraced	5
Devils Dance	32
Drafted Sorrow	67
Electric Song	72
Escalators	71
Evolution	16
Eyes That Smile	3
False Hopes	18
First Snow	38
Fonts Baptismaux	7
Foundations of Silence	56
Hidden	21
I Starve	64
In Memory	11
Inhalation of Yesterday	6
Journey	19
Lament	51
Maelstrom	78
Mesmerism	60

Myopic	17
Myself	53
Nocturnal	13
On Nil's Beach	68
Past	15
Photo Fragments	9
Quick Winter Visit	54
Recluse	63
Returning	70
Reverie	30
Rigor Mortis	76
Scattered Thoughts	8
Some Blues	66
Song to Her Dusk	35
Songs of Soft Map Readings	55
Spoken	20
The Golden Fleece	10
The Mind at Night Moments	40
The Next Corner Turned	50
The Shifting-Time of My Own Psyche	29
The Uncontemplative	12
Thorns	22
Triad From Past Prose	36
Vertigo in June	62
Village Vagrant	34

www.ingramcontent.com/pod-product-compliance
Lightning Source LLC
Chambersburg PA
CBHW031654040426
42453CB00006B/307